Let's Talk About
Going to the Dentist

Marianne Johnston

Heinemann
L I B R A R Y

First published in Great Britain by Heinemann Library,
Halley Court, Jordan Hill, Oxford OX2 8EJ,
a division of Reed Educational & Professional Publishing Ltd.

OXFORD FLORENCE PRAGUE MADRID ATHENS MELBOURNE AUCKLAND
KUALA LUMPUR SINGAPORE TOKYO IBADAN NAIROBI KAMPALA JOHANNESBURG GABORONE
PORTSMOUTH NH (USA) CHICAGO MEXICO CITY SAO PAOLO

Manufactured in the United States of America

02 01 00 99 98
10 9 8 7 6 5 4 3 2 1
ISBN 0431 03601 2

British Library Cataloguing in Publication Data
Johnston, Marianne
Let's talk about going to the dentist
1. Dental clinics - Juvenile literature 2. Dentistry - Juvenile literature
I. Title II. Going to the dentist
617.6

Acknowledgements
The Publishers would like to thank the following for permission to reproduce photographs:
All photos by Seth Dinnerman
Our thanks to Mandy Ross in the preparation of this edition.
Every effort has been made to contact copyright holders of any material reproduced in this book.
Any omissions will be rectified in subsequent printings if notice is given to the Publisher.

Contents

Words in **bold letters like these** are explained in the Glossary on page 23.

Teeth are important

Lots of people hate brushing their teeth. But teeth need to be taken care of, just like the rest of our bodies.

Imagine what life would be like if you didn't have any teeth. You couldn't chew your food. You couldn't speak well, because your teeth help you to speak clearly. If we don't take good care of our teeth, they get unhealthy and they may even fall out. The dentist helps us to keep our teeth healthy.

◀ We need our teeth in order to eat crunchy foods like apples.

What is a dentist?

A dentist is a doctor who knows all about what's inside your mouth. The mouth is the only part of the body a dentist works on. He or she knows all about your teeth and whether they are healthy or not.

If your teeth are healthy, the dentist just cleans them. If they are not healthy, the dentist knows how to make them stronger. He or she can also show you how to take better care of them.

Dentists are specially trained to work on people's mouths. ▶

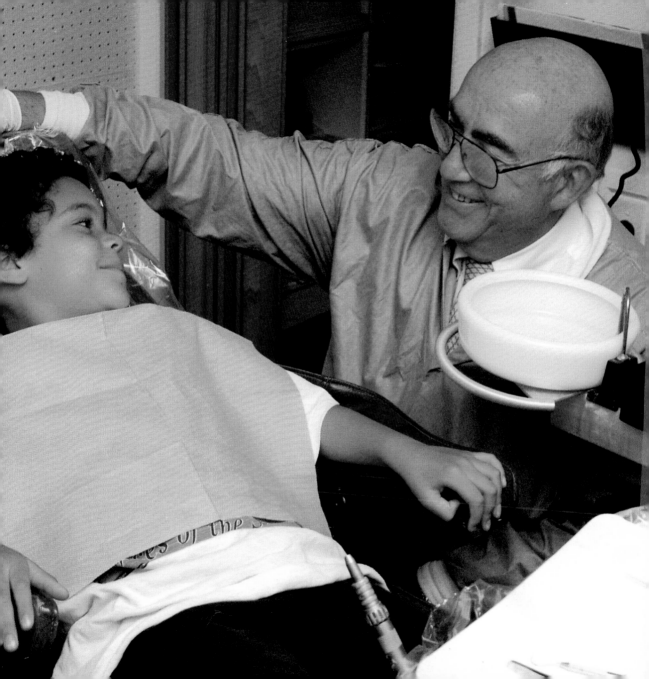

In the waiting room

When you first get to the dentist's **surgery**, you will have to wait in a waiting room. Your parents may have to fill in some forms. These will tell the dentist who you are and whether you've been there before.

Most waiting rooms have magazines or books to read while you wait. There may even be toys to play with. But you may want to bring your favourite book or toy, just in case.

If you're nervous while you're waiting, tell your mum. She can explain what will happen when you see the dentist.

The dentist's helpers

The dental nurse works with the dentist. When your name is called, the dental nurse will help you into the dentist's big, comfortable chair. You can almost lie down in it. It also moves up and down. The nurse may put a paper towel around your neck to keep your clothes dry.

The **hygienist** also works with the dentist. He or she knows how to clean your teeth really thoroughly.

The nurse makes sure you are comfortable before the dentist starts work. ▶

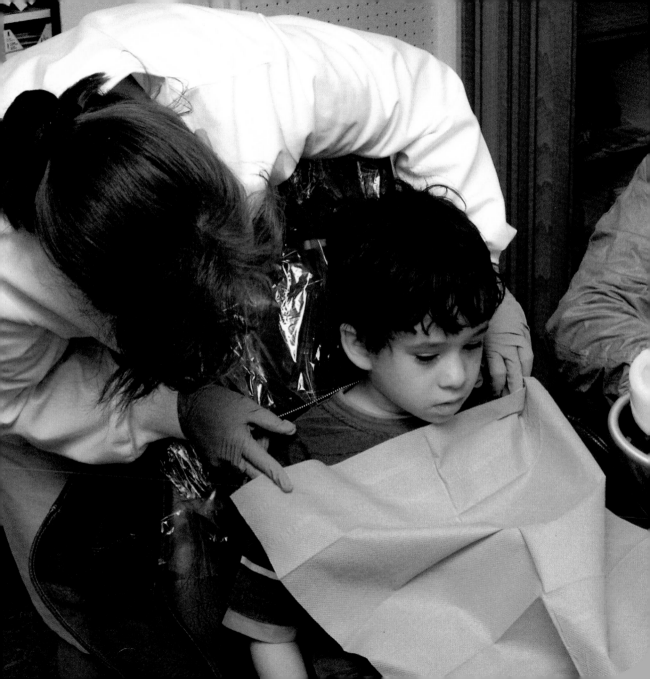

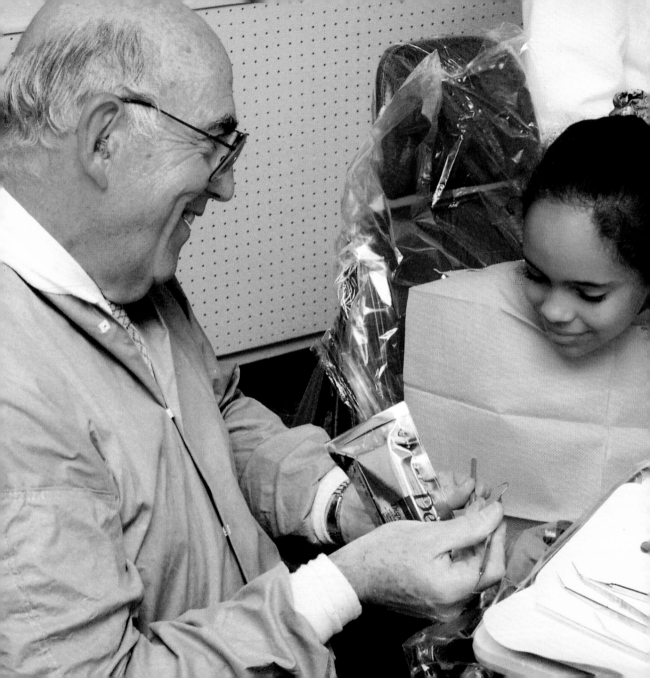

The dentist

The dentist examines your teeth and **gums** to make sure they are healthy. Then the dentist, or sometimes the **hygienist**, will give your teeth a very good cleaning.

He or she uses a special cleaning tool with a smooth rubber tip that spins round quickly. The spinning tip rubs away all the food and **plaque** (left-over food and germs) from your teeth. Sometimes it tickles, but it doesn't hurt at all.

◀ Don't be afraid to ask to see the dentist's tools and how they work.

Special tools

Dentists and **hygienists** use special tools to check and clean your teeth. One is a small metal tool, about the size of a pencil, with a hook at the end. The dentist uses the hook to check your teeth and to clean gently around and between them.

Dentists use a small rubber **suction** tube to suck away the **saliva**, or spit, from your mouth. This makes your mouth dry, which feels funny. But it makes it easier for the dentist to work.

The dentist keeps all the tools on a small tray. ▶

Cavities and fillings

A **cavity** is a hollow where the tooth has become soft. If you have a cavity, the dentist uses a drill to get rid of the soft part of the tooth, and then fills the hole with a hard material called a **filling**. Then your tooth is as good as new.

The dentist may give you an **injection**, or jab, so that the drilling won't hurt. The injection may sting, but afterwards you won't feel anything until the dentist has finished.

The dentist may take an x-ray, or a photograph, of your teeth to see if you have any cavities.

Wearing a brace

If your teeth are growing crooked, you may need to wear a **brace**. A brace is made of metal or plastic wires and bands. The dentist fits it onto your teeth, and slowly it moves your teeth into the right place.

A brace may make your mouth a bit sore sometimes. You might have to avoid foods which get stuck in it. And you must brush your teeth carefully. But when the brace comes off, you will have a great smile.

Wearing a brace may feel odd at first, but you will get used to it.

Advice from the dentist

After your check-up, the dentist will show you how to brush your teeth properly, and how to use **dental floss**. Dental floss is a waxy thread that you slide between your teeth to get rid of food and **plaque** trapped there.

The dentist may tell you to eat foods, such as cheese, that are rich in **calcium**. This will help your teeth to stay healthy. Sweets and sugar are bad for your teeth.

Foods with calcium, such as milk and cheese, are good for your teeth.

Time to go home

Before you leave, you can book another check-up. Your check-ups should be about every six months. Regular visits to the dentist will keep your teeth strong and healthy, and give you a beautiful smile.

Glossary

brace (BRAYSS) – metal or plastic wires and bands used to straighten crooked teeth

calcium (KAL-see-um) – foods rich in calcium help to keep your teeth and bones strong

cavity (KA-vi-tee) – hole or soft spot in a tooth

dental floss – strong thread for cleaning between teeth

filling – hard material that fills a hole or **cavity** in a tooth

gum – the firm flesh around your teeth

hygienist (hi-JEEN-ist) – dentist's helper who cleans your teeth

injection (in-JEK-shun) – a jab with a dentist's needle

plaque (PLAK) – a thin covering of germs and food that forms on teeth and can cause cavities

saliva (sa-LY-va) – spit, or liquid in the mouth that keeps the mouth moist and helps to make chewing easier

suction (SUK-shun) – sucking away air or liquid

surgery (SUR-jer-ree) – where a dentist or doctor works

Index